Vintage Botany Botanical Flower Prints Volume 2 (Floral Ephemera Series 2)
By C. Anders

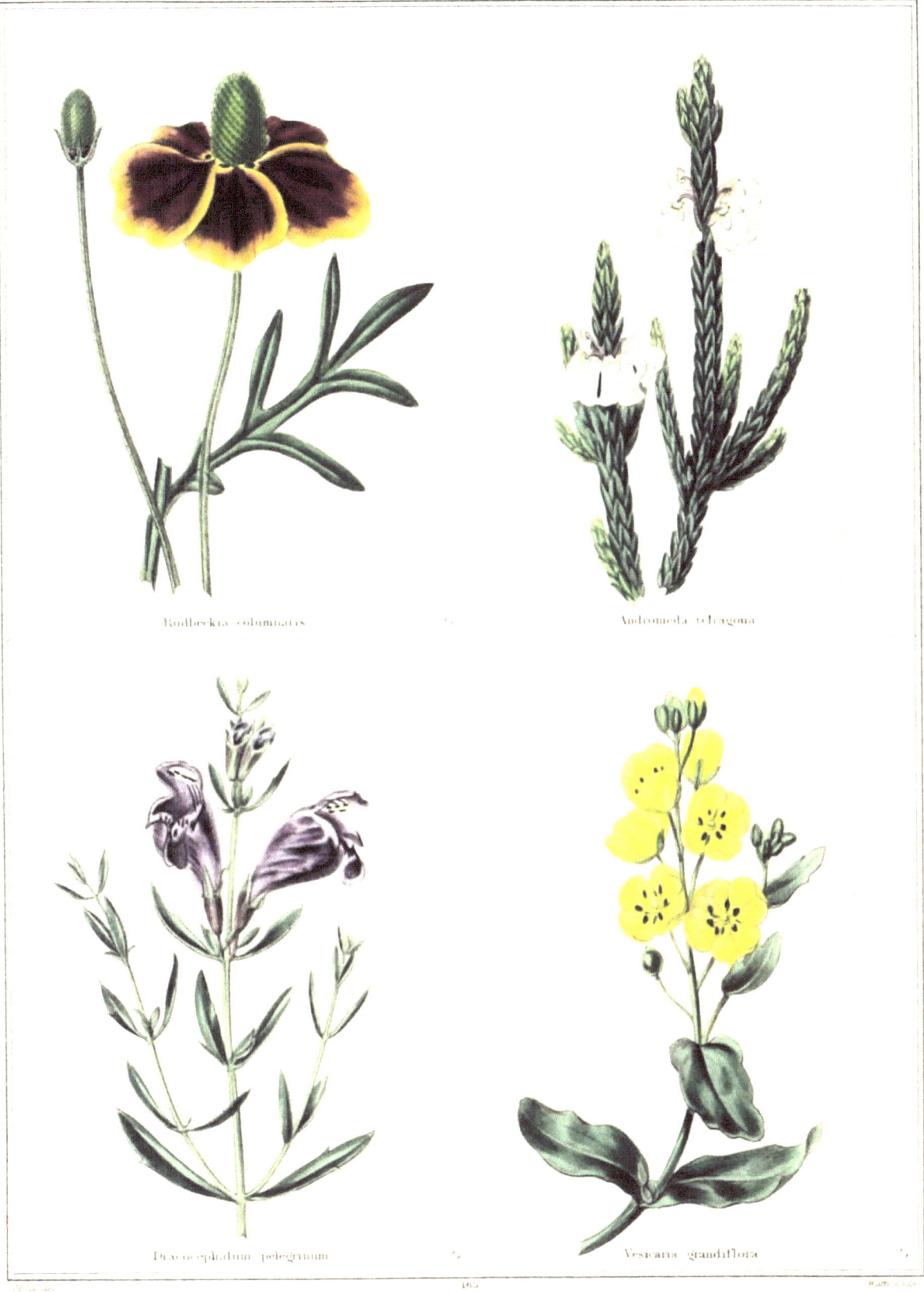

Rudbeckia columnaris

Andromeda tetragona

Dracocephalum peregrinum

Vesicaria grandiflora

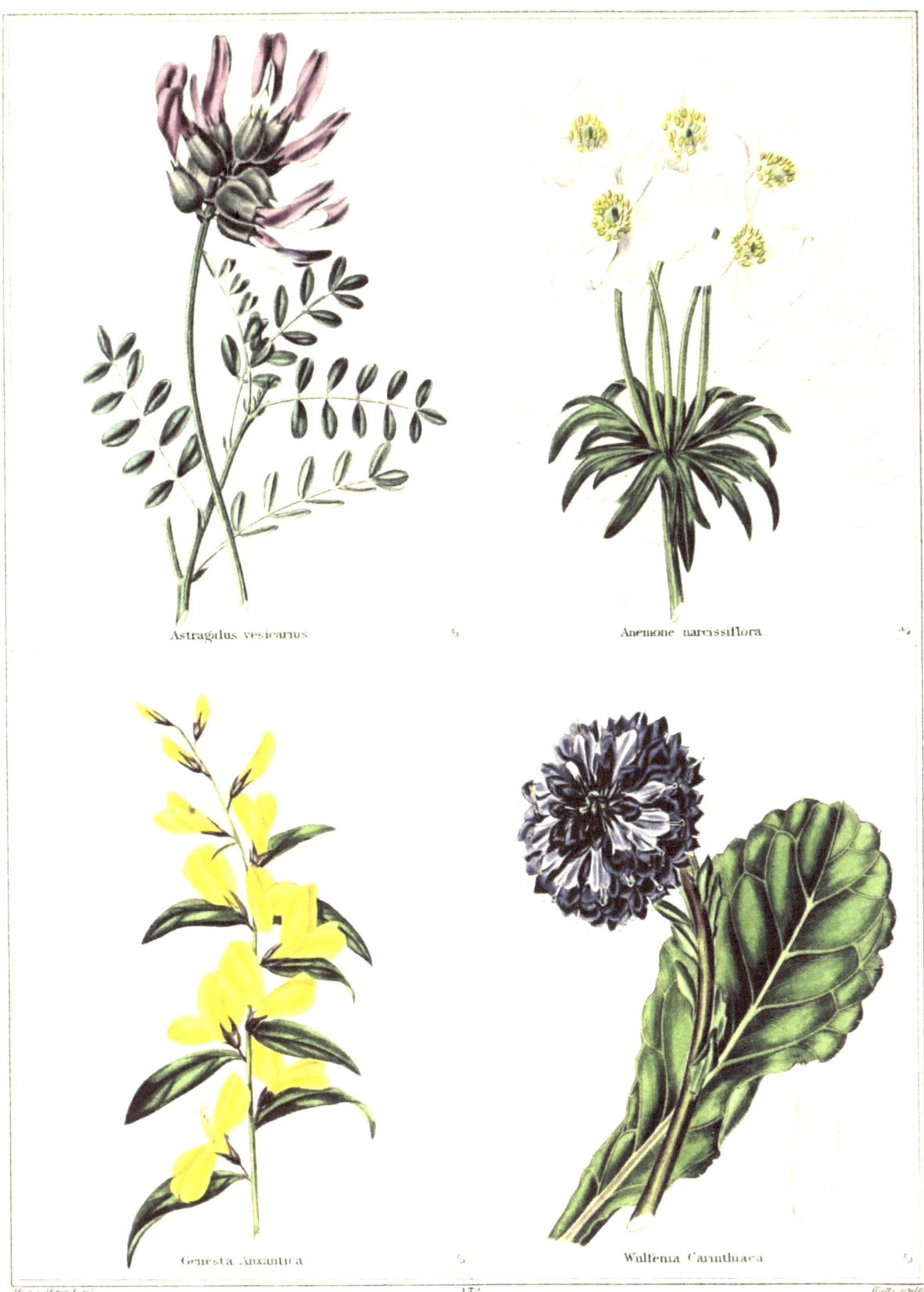

Astragalus vesicarius

Anemone narcissiflora.

Genista Anxantica

Wulfenia Carinthiaca

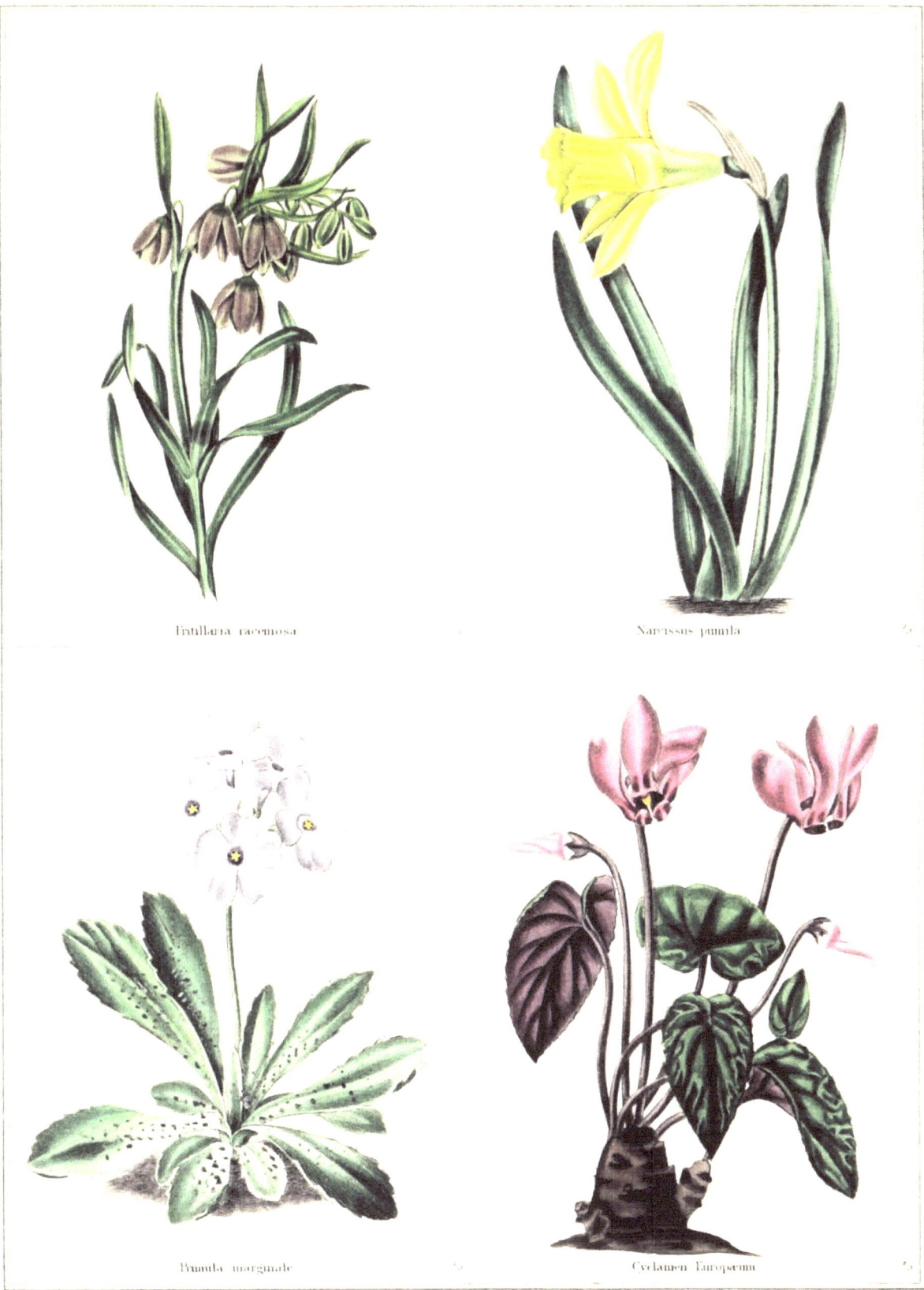

Fritillaria racemosa

Narcissus pumila

Primula marginale

Cyclamen Europaeum

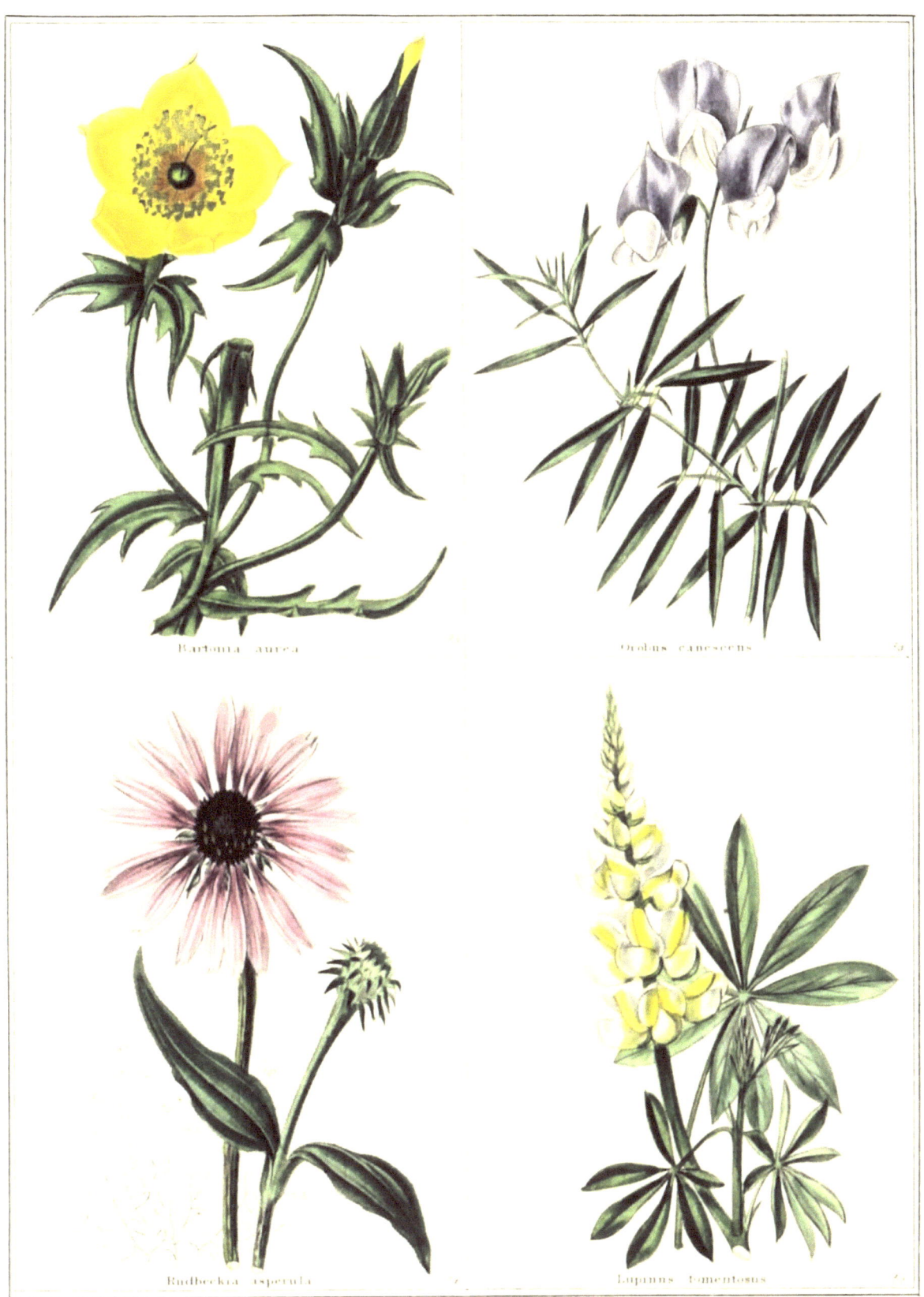

Bartonia aurea

Orobus canescens

Rudbeckia aspernula

Lupinus tomentosus

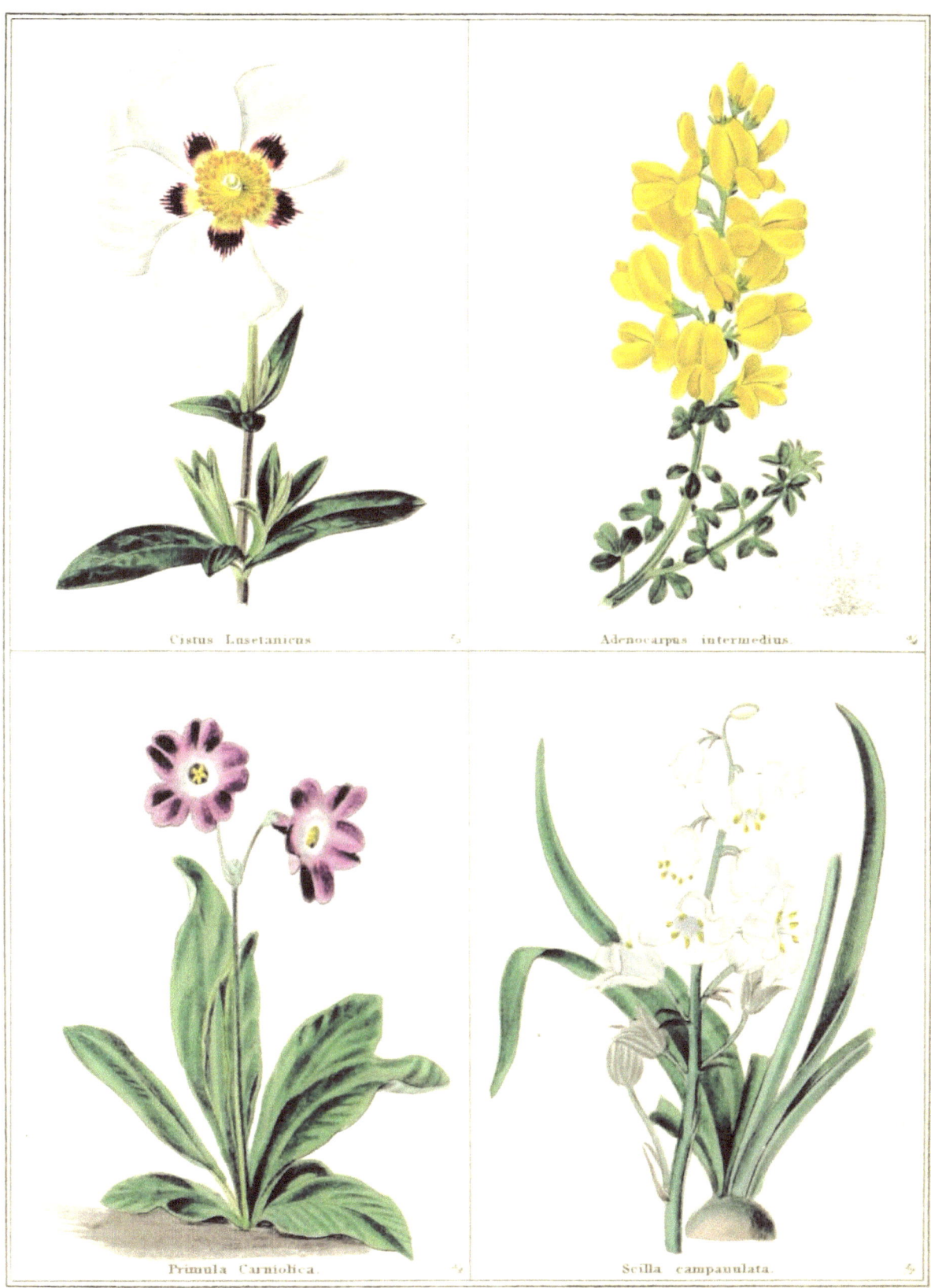

Cistus Lusetanicus

Adenocarpus intermedius.

Primula Carniolica.

Scilla campauulata.

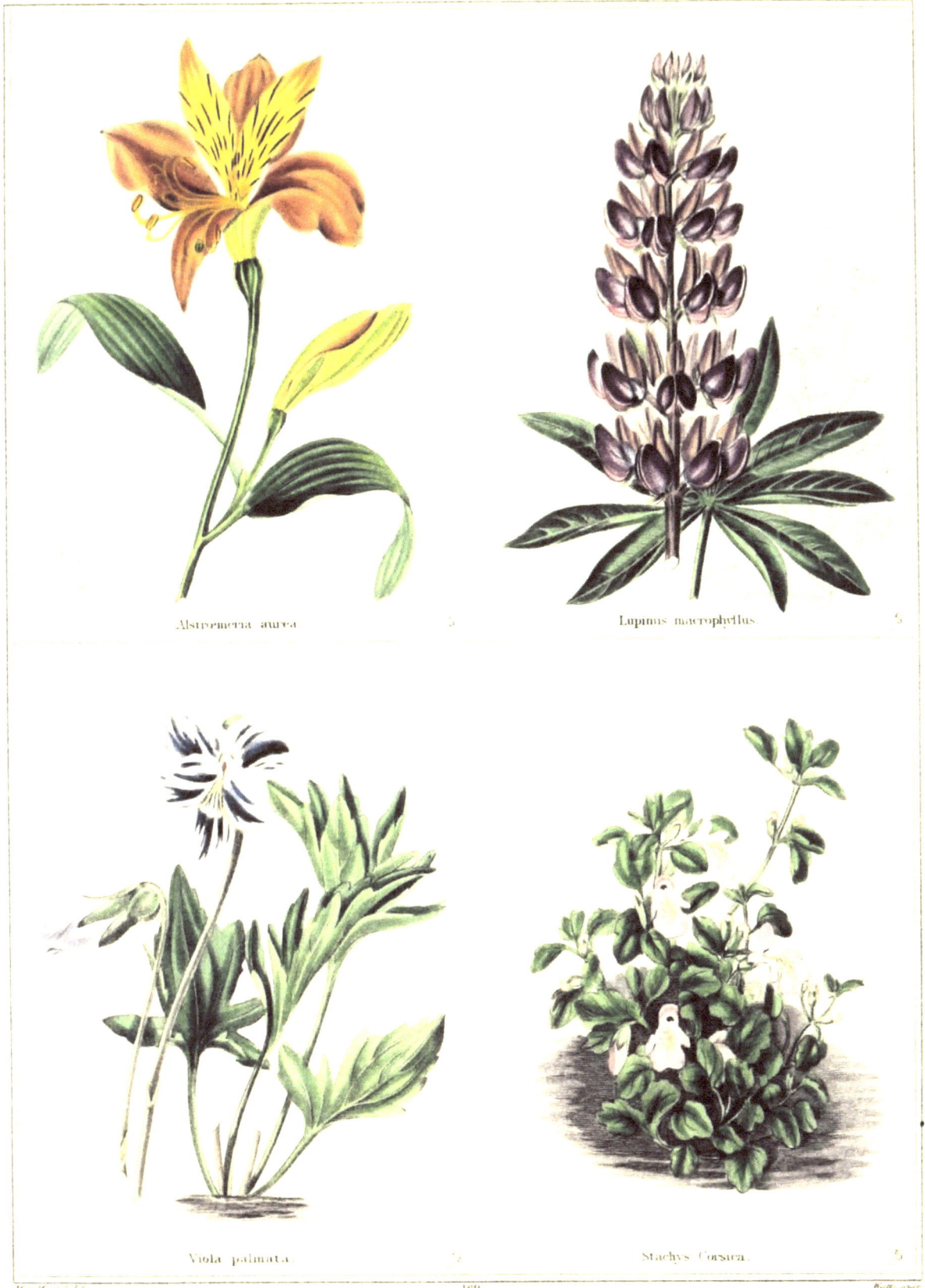

Alstroemeria aurea

Lupinus macrophyllus

Viola palmata

Stachys Corsica

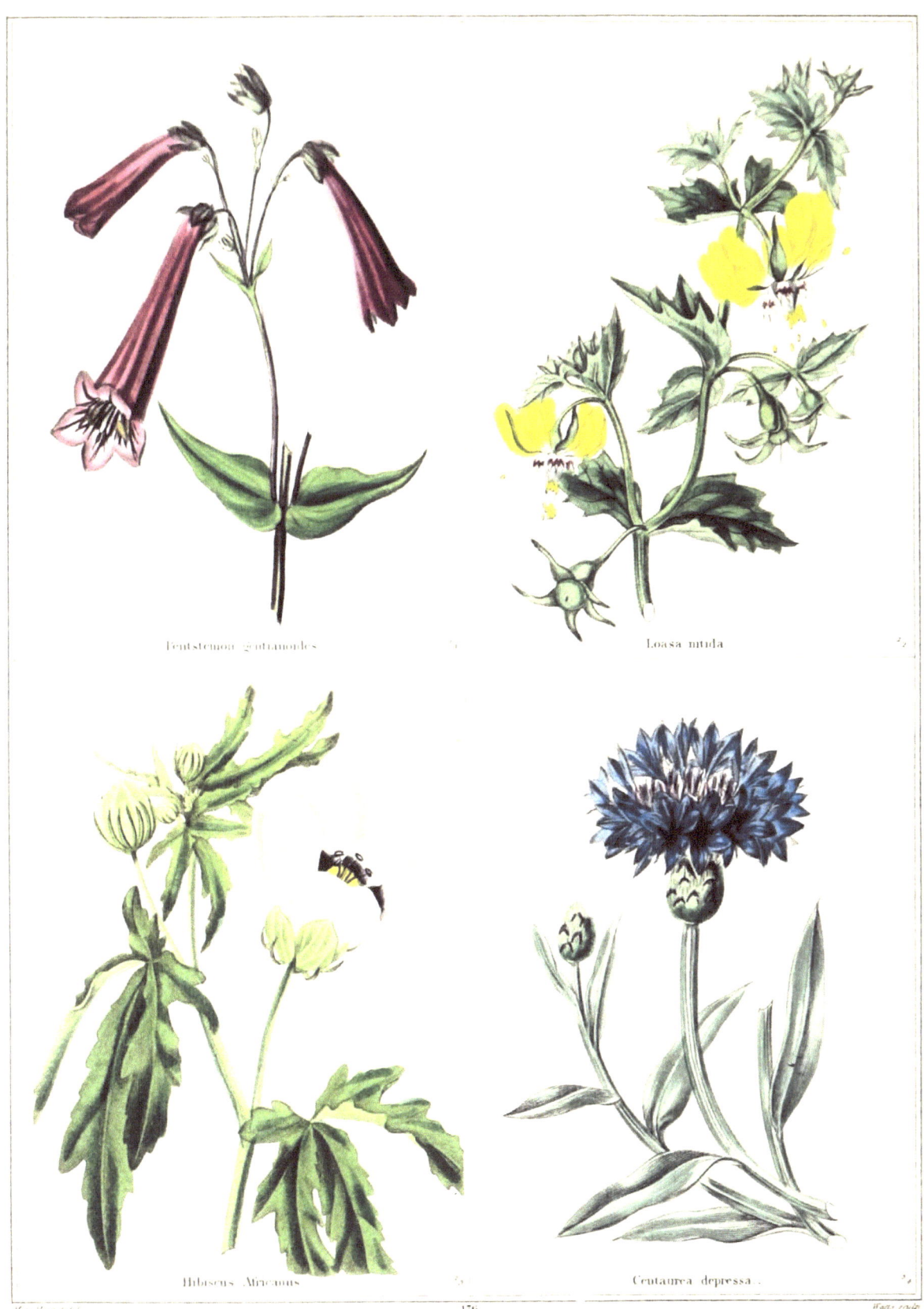

Pentstemon gentianoides.

Loasa nitida

Hibiscus Africanus

Centaurea depressa.

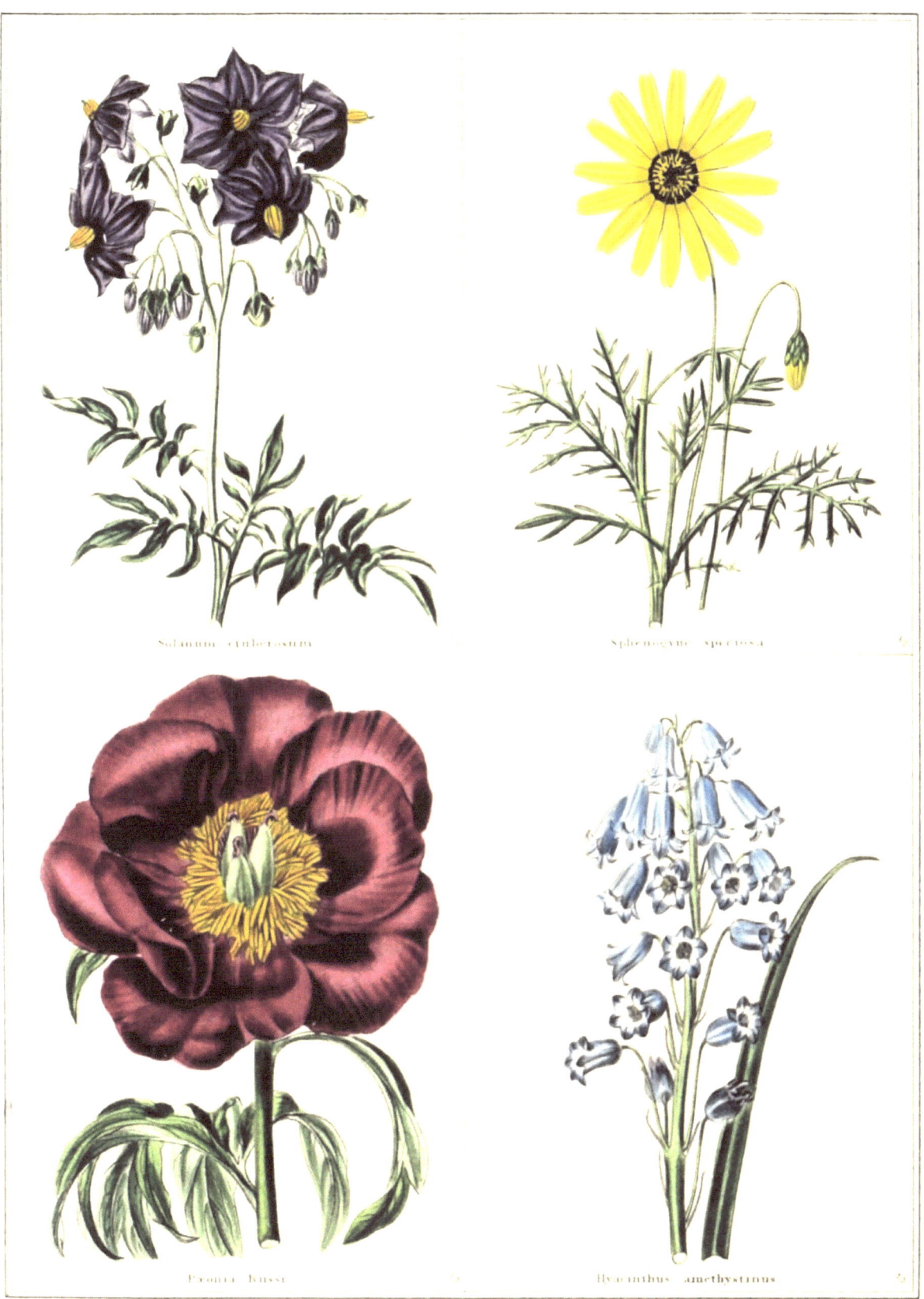

Solanum tuberosum

Sphenogyne speciosa

Prœnia Russi

Hyacinthus amethystinus

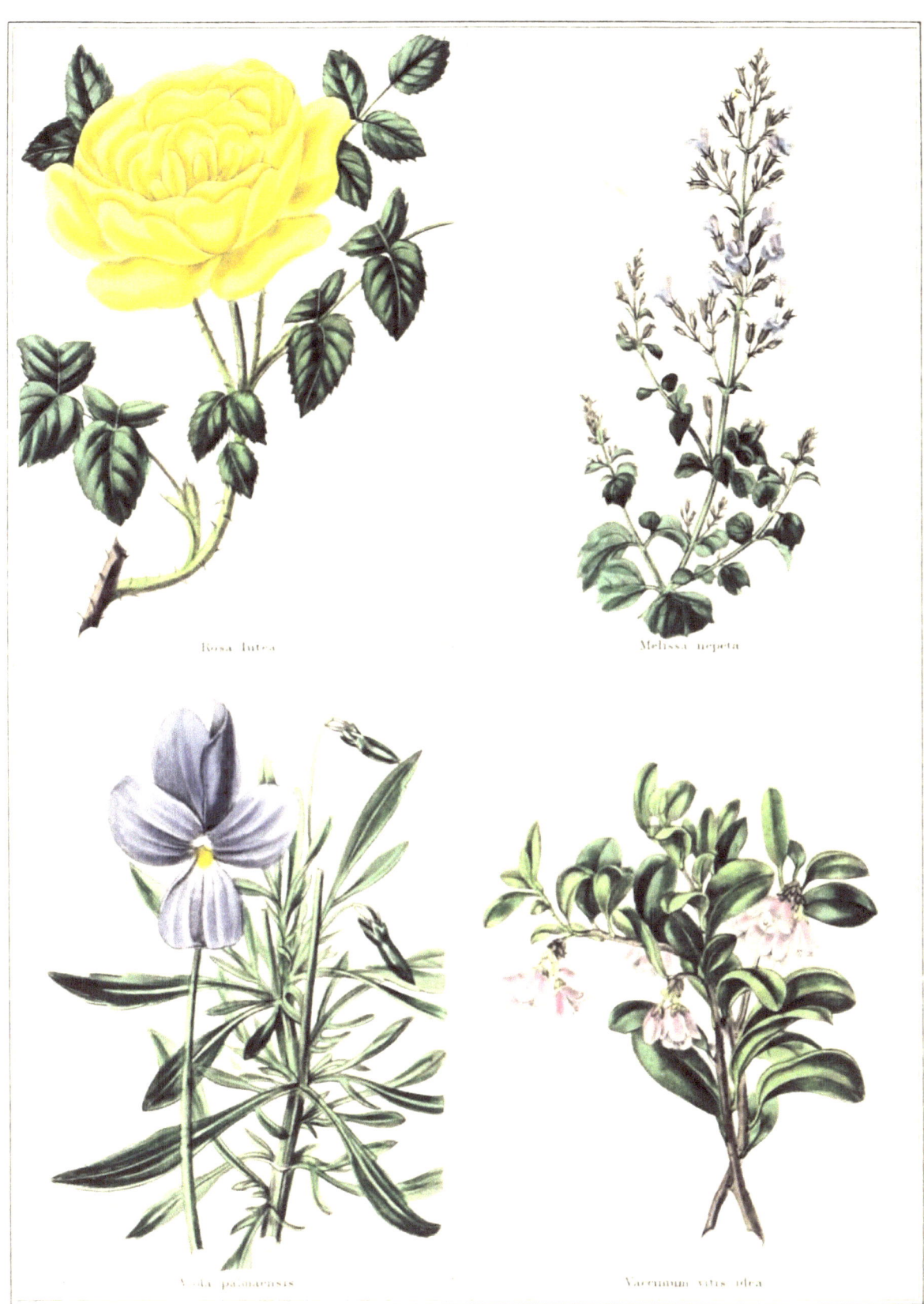

Rosa lutea

Melissa nepeta

Viola parmaensis

Vaccinium vitis-idea

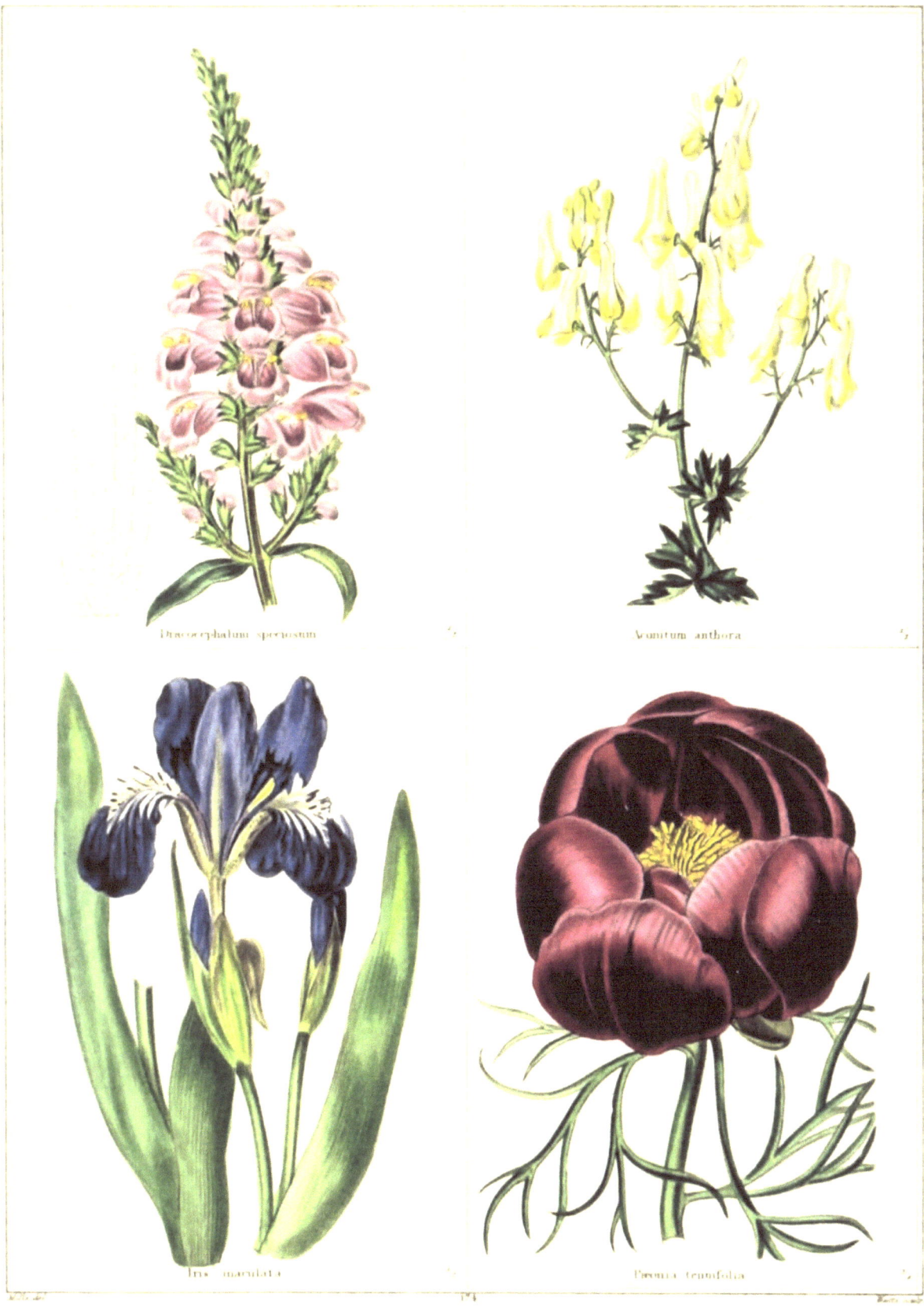

Dracocephalum speciosum

Aconitum anthora

Iris maculata

Pæonia tenuifolia

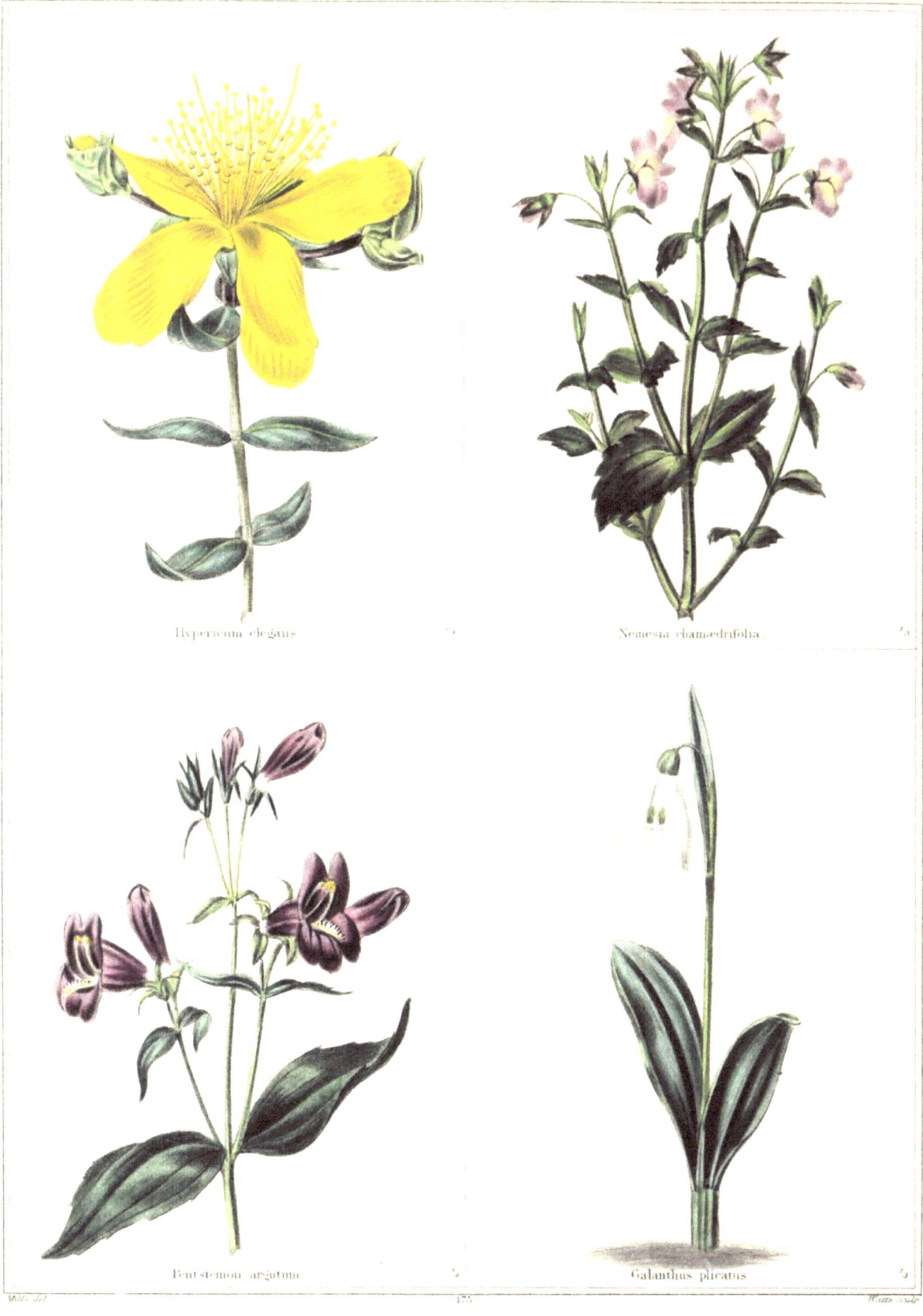

Hypericum elegans

Nemesia chamædrifolia

Pentstemon argutum

Galanthus plicatus

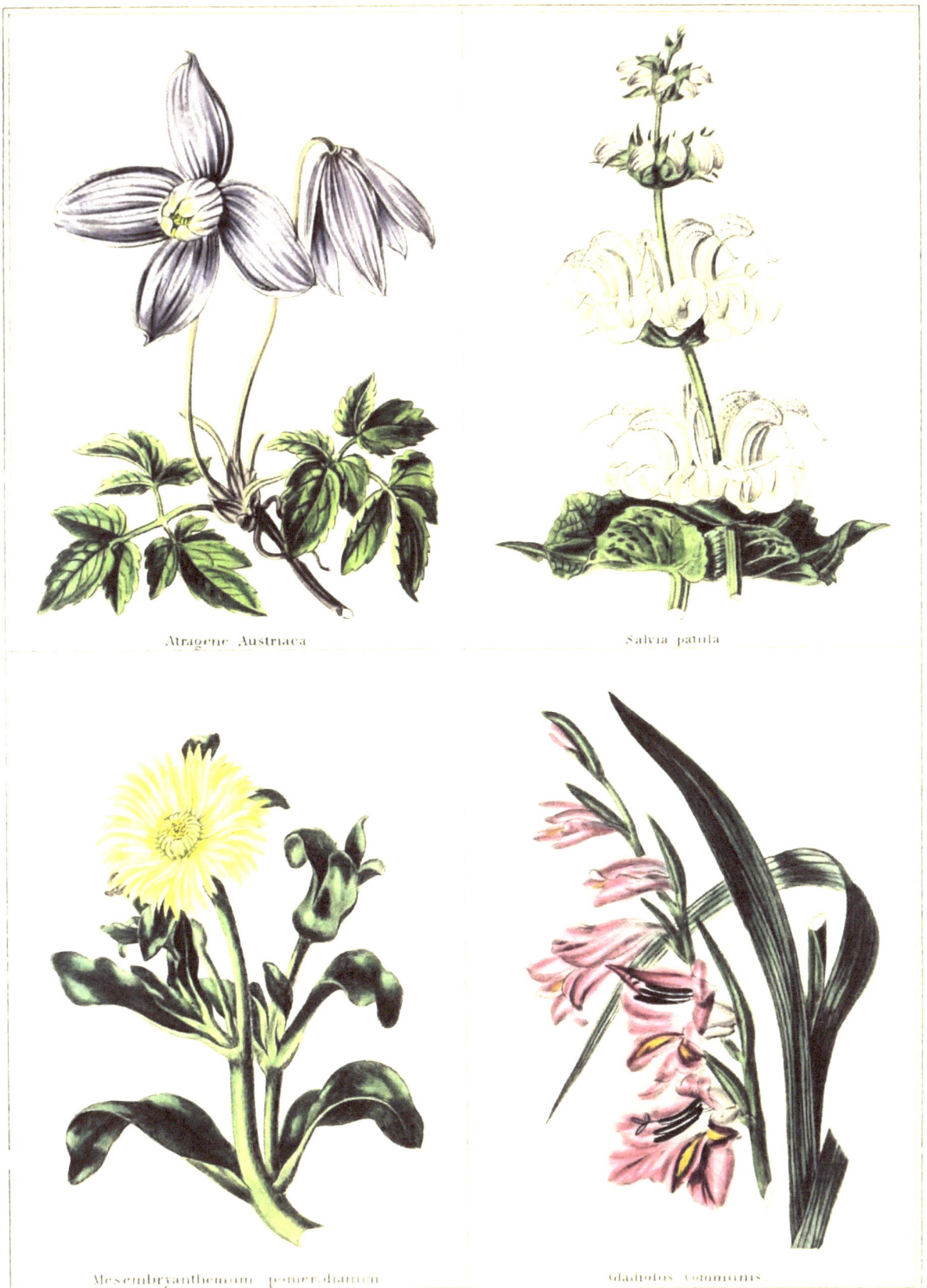

Atragene Austriaca

Salvia patula

Mesembryanthemum pomeridianum

Gladiolus Communis

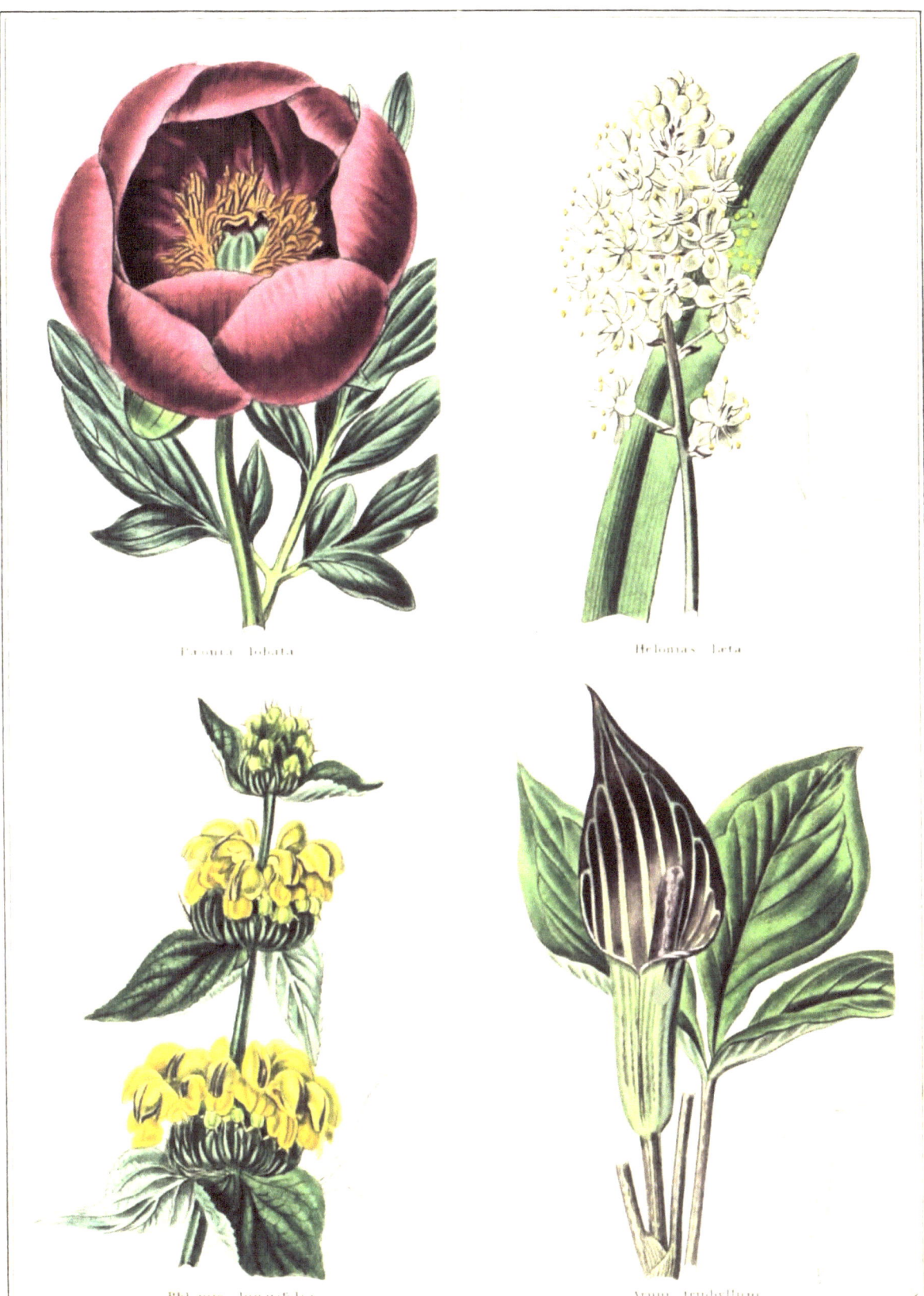

Paeonia lobata

Helonias leta

Phlomis lunarifolia

Arum triphyllum

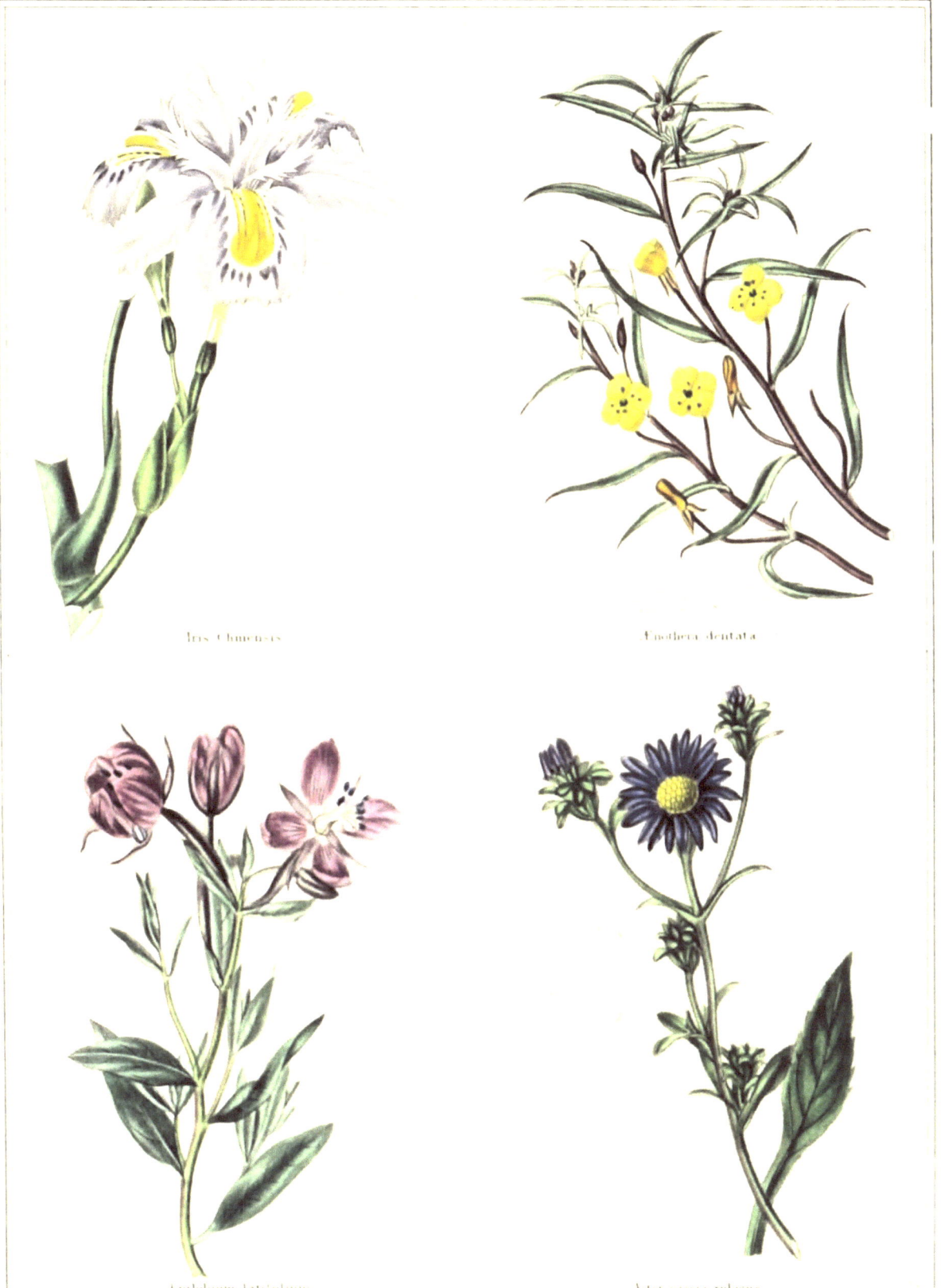

Iris Chinensis

Œnothera dentata

Epilobium latifolium

Aster cassu rubens

105

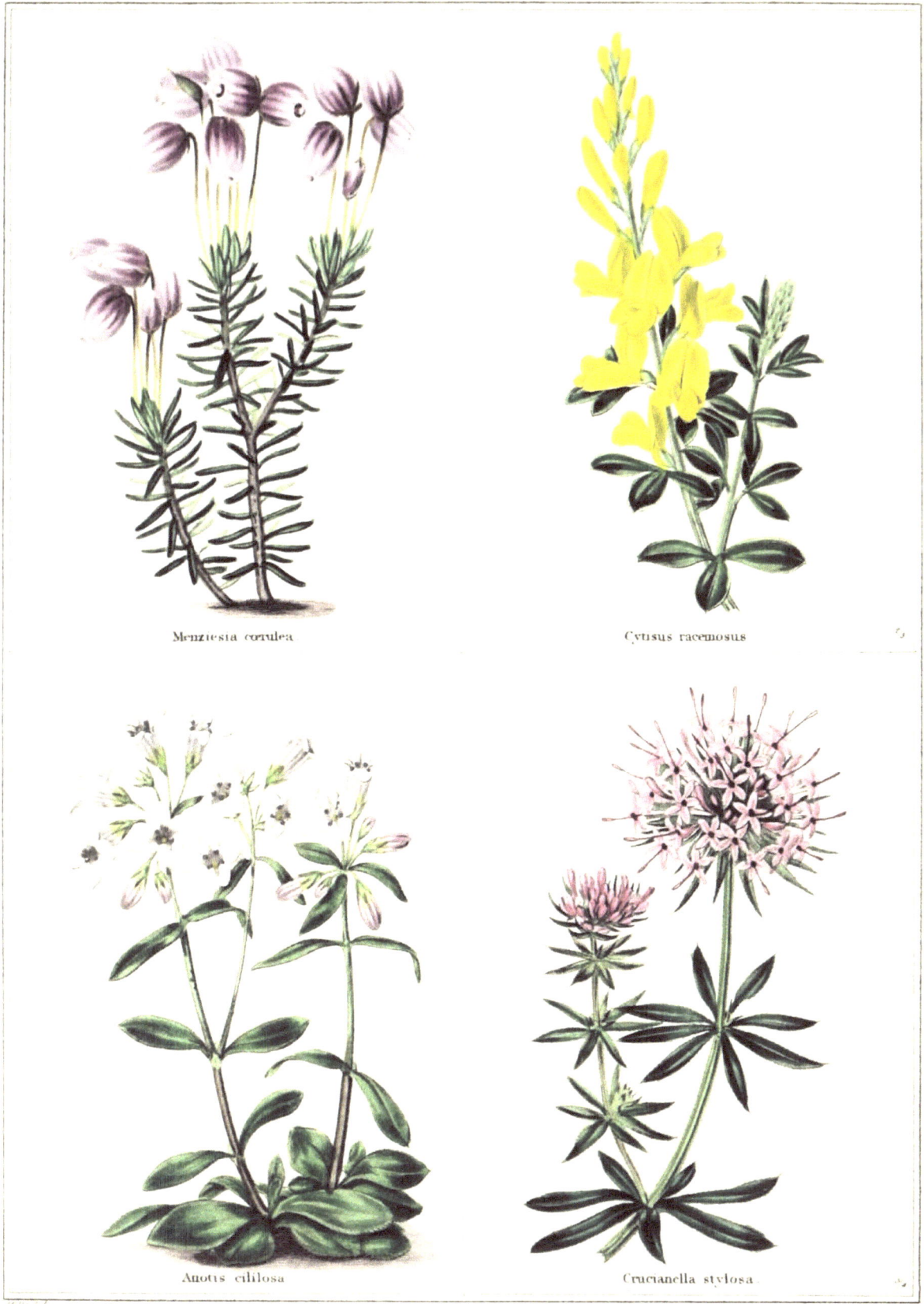

Menziesia cœrulea

Cytisus racemosus

Anotis cililosa

Crucianella stylosa

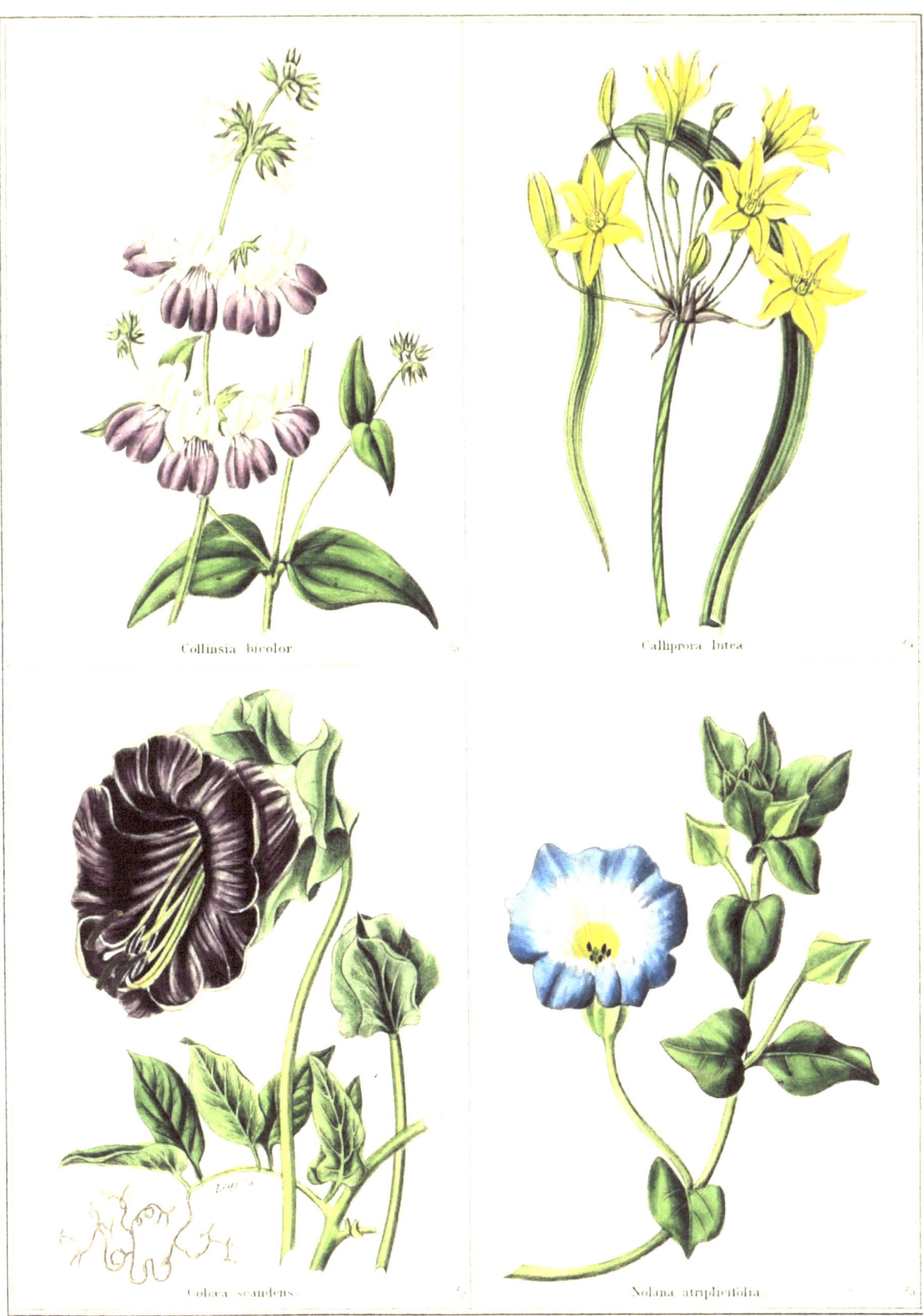

Collinsia bicolor.

Calliprora lutea.

Cobæa scandens.

Nolana atriplicifolia.

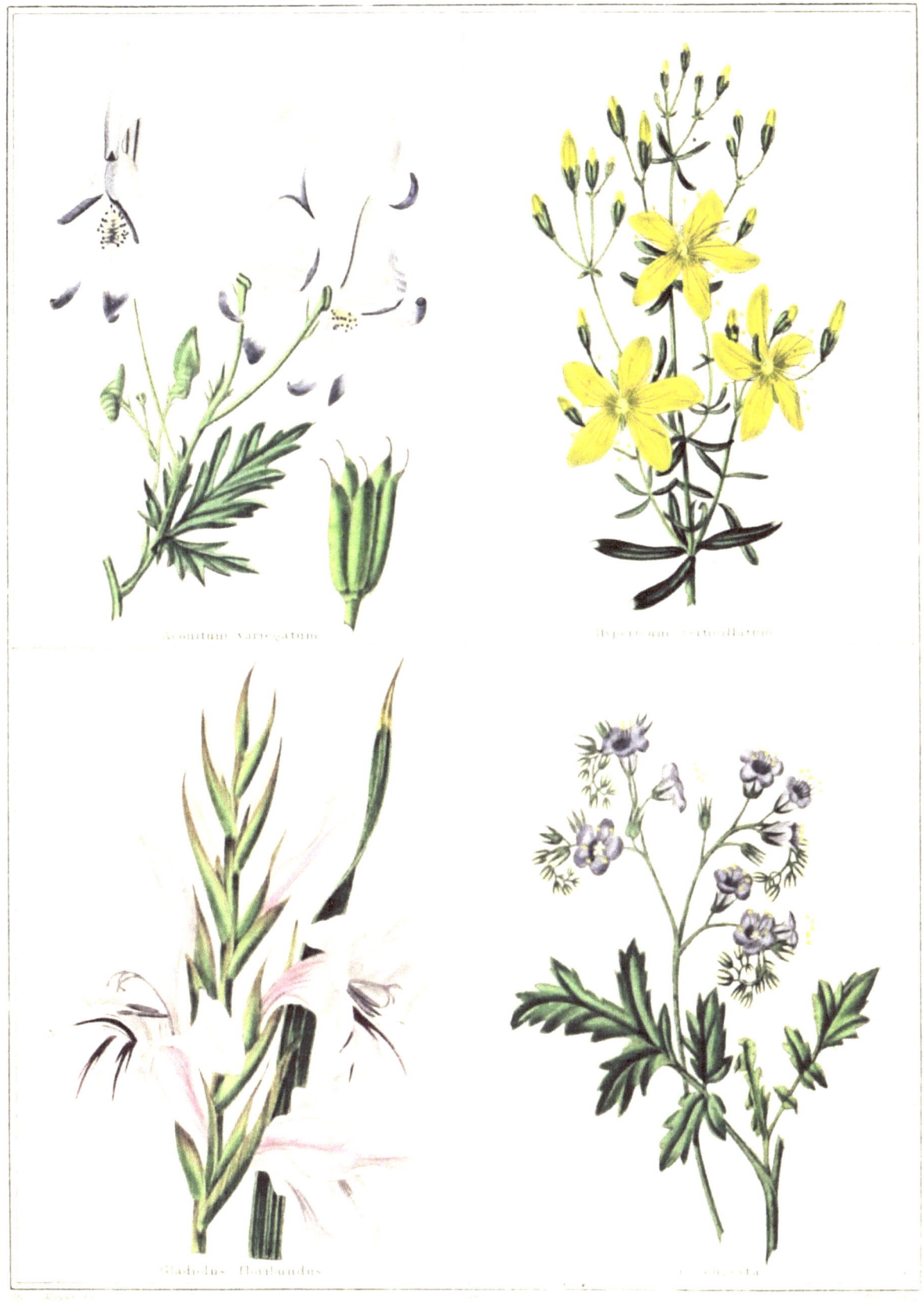

Aconitum variegatum

Hypericum verticillatum

Gladiolus floribundus

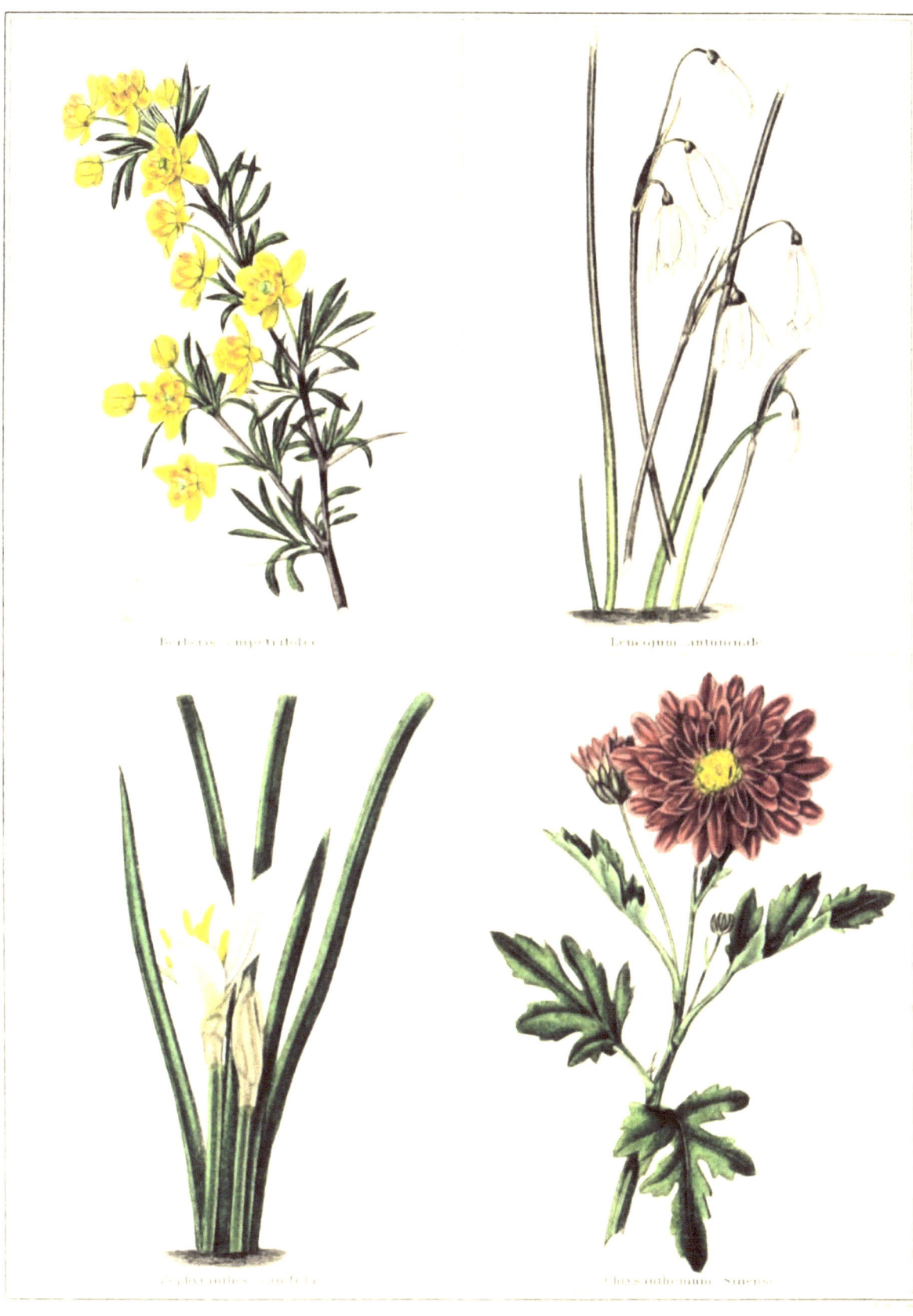

Berberis empetrifolia

Leucojum autumnale

Cyclanthus conchita

Chrysanthemum Sinense

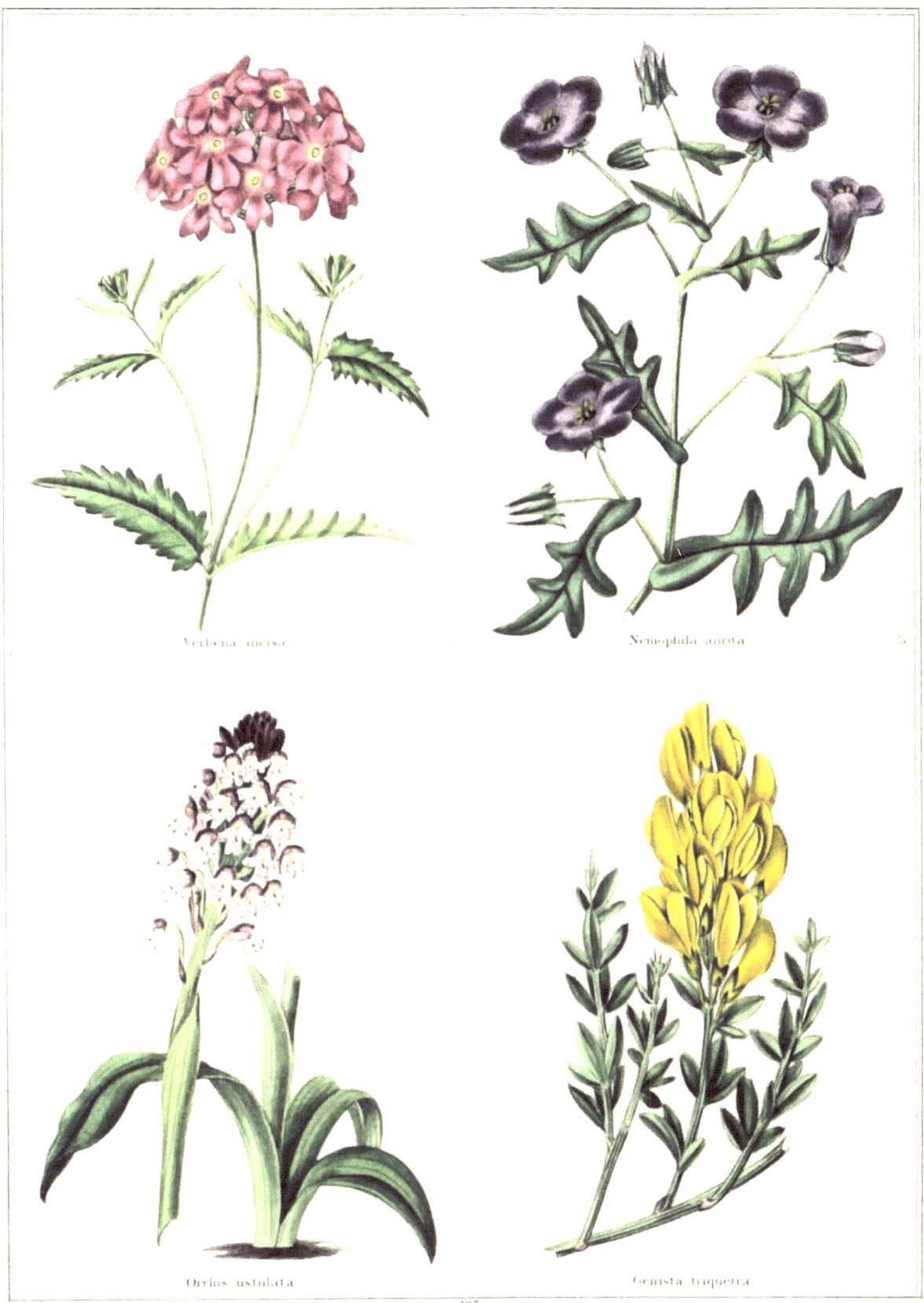

Verbena incisa

Nemophila aurita

Orchis ustulata

Genista triquetra

167

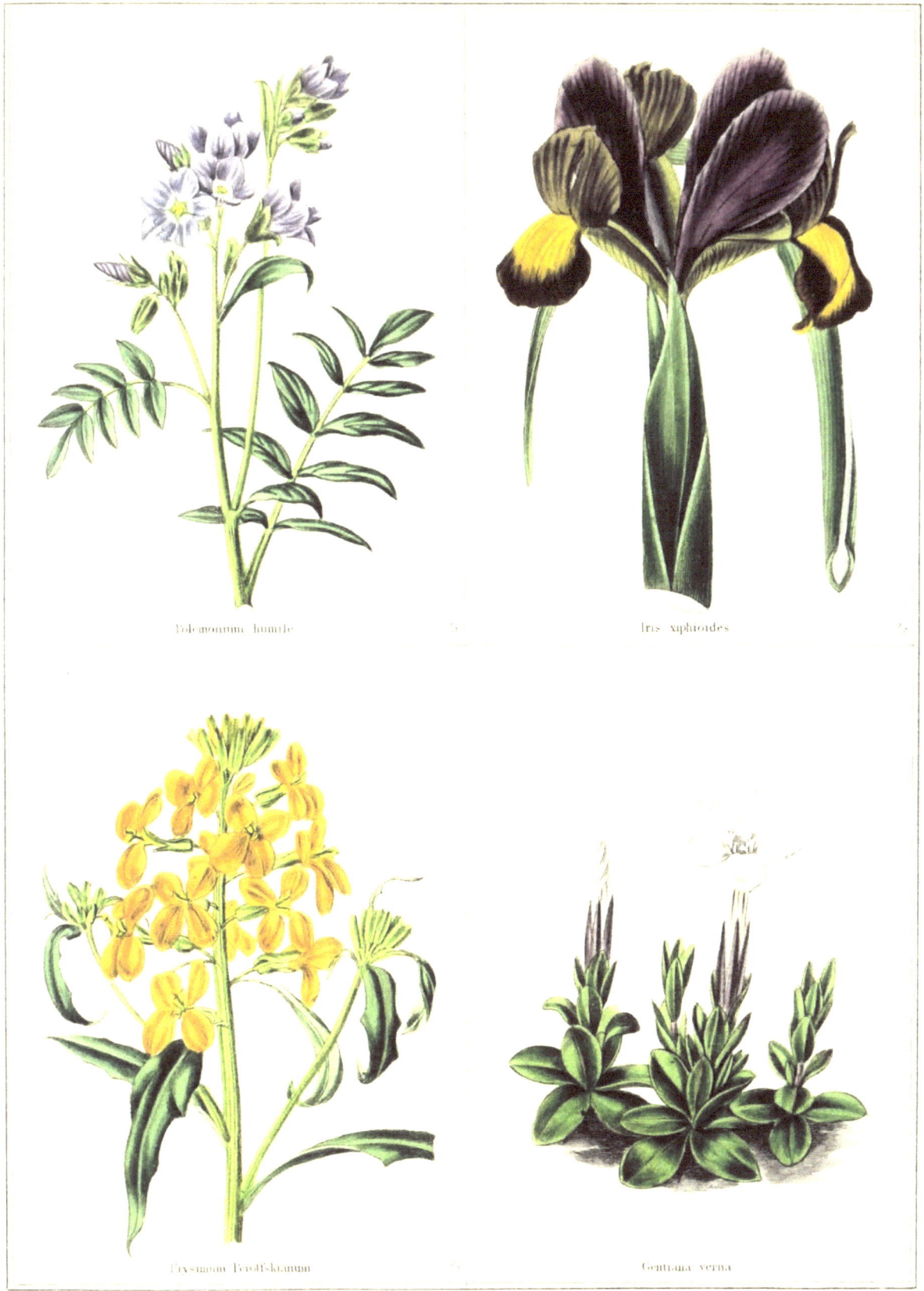

Polemonium humile

Iris xiphioides

Erysimum Perofiskianum

Gentiana verna

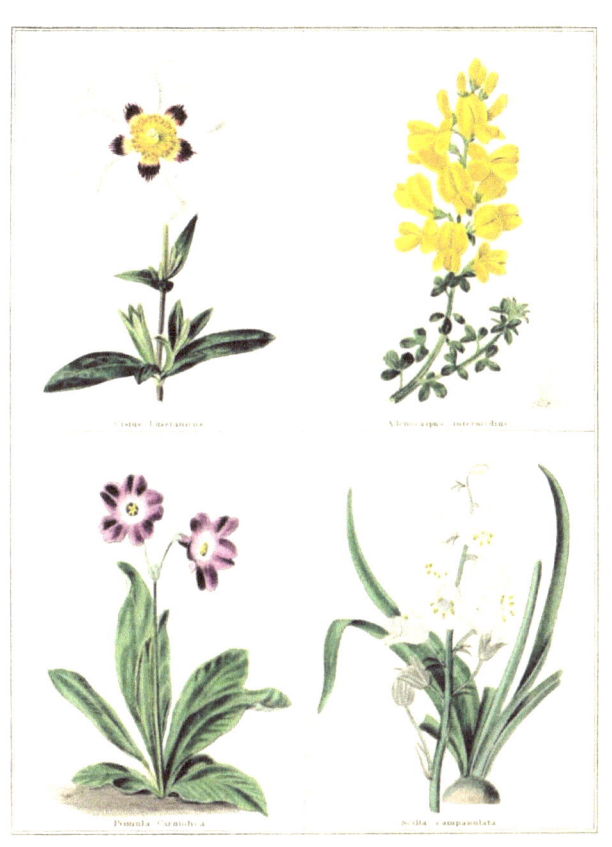

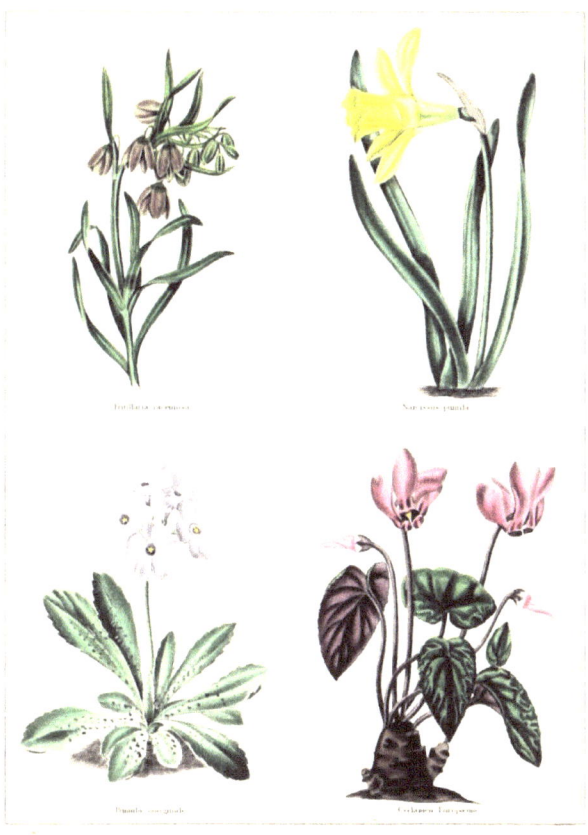

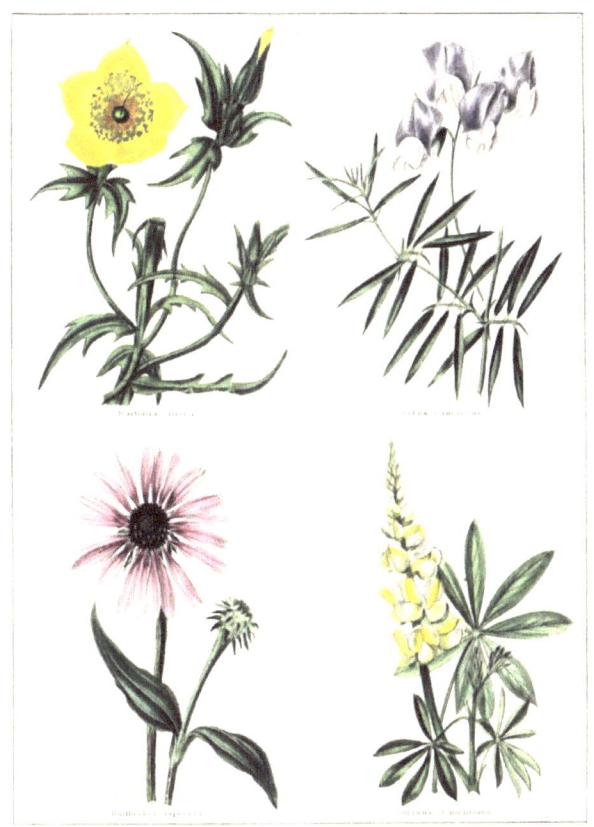

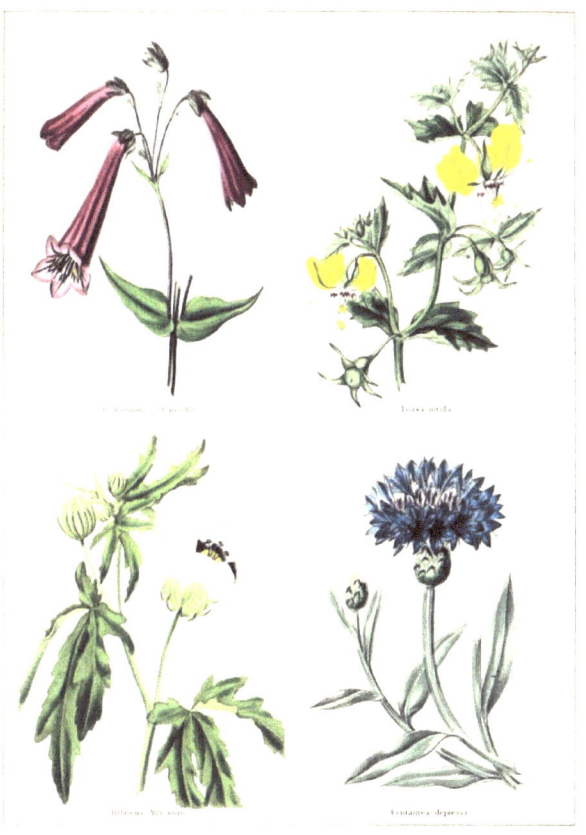

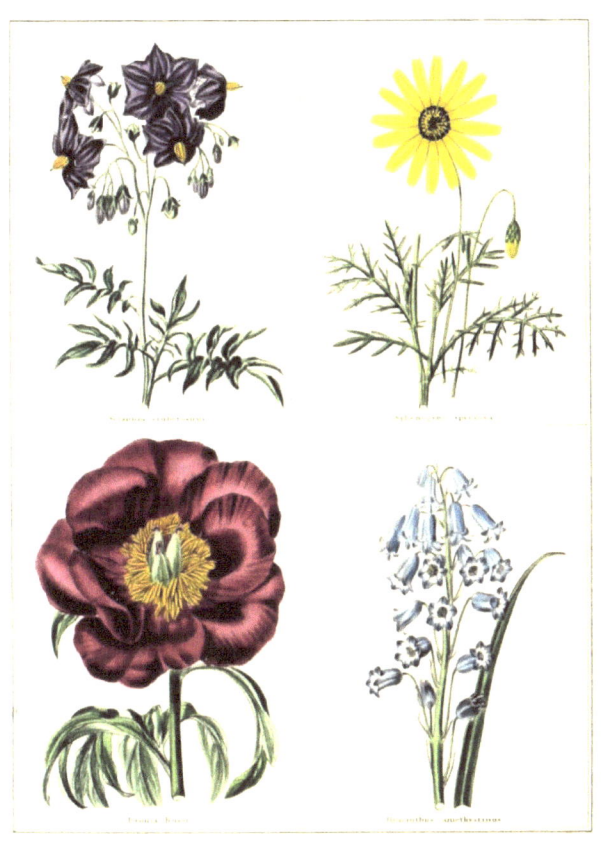

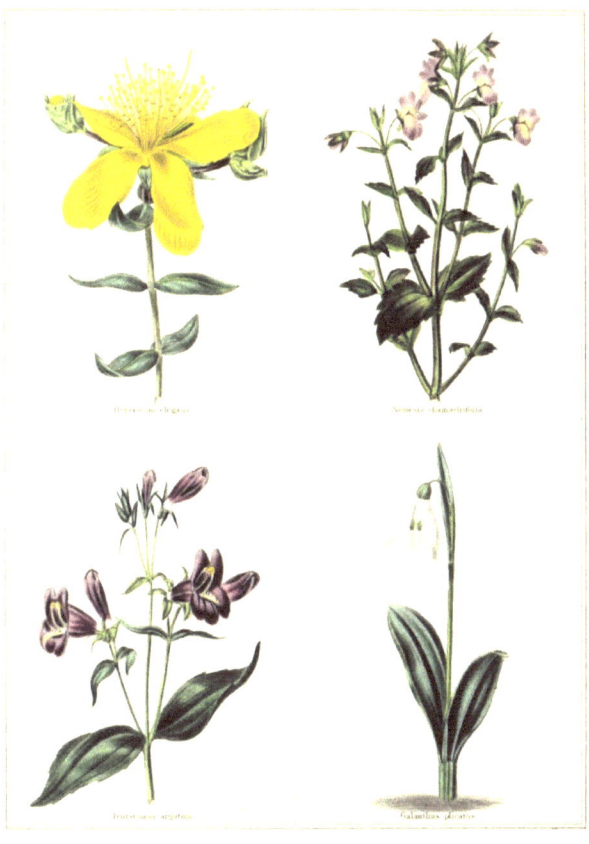

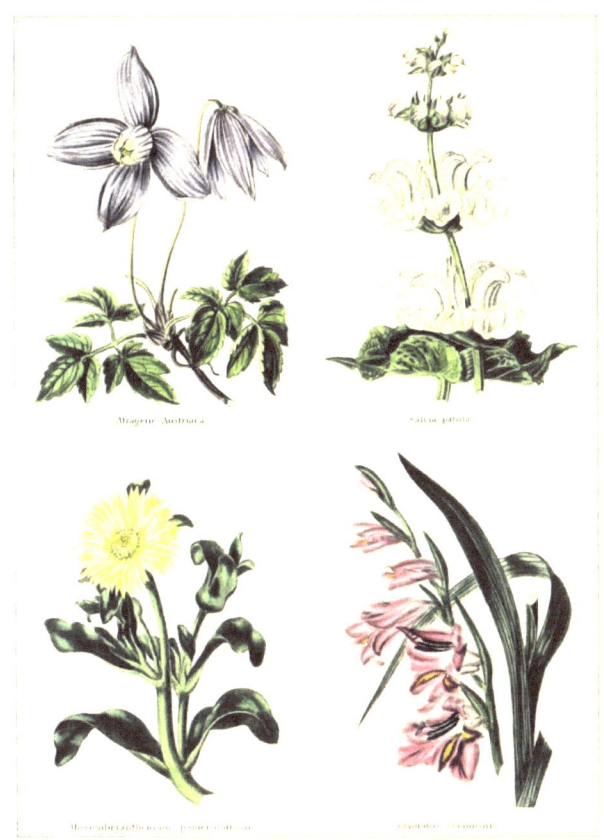

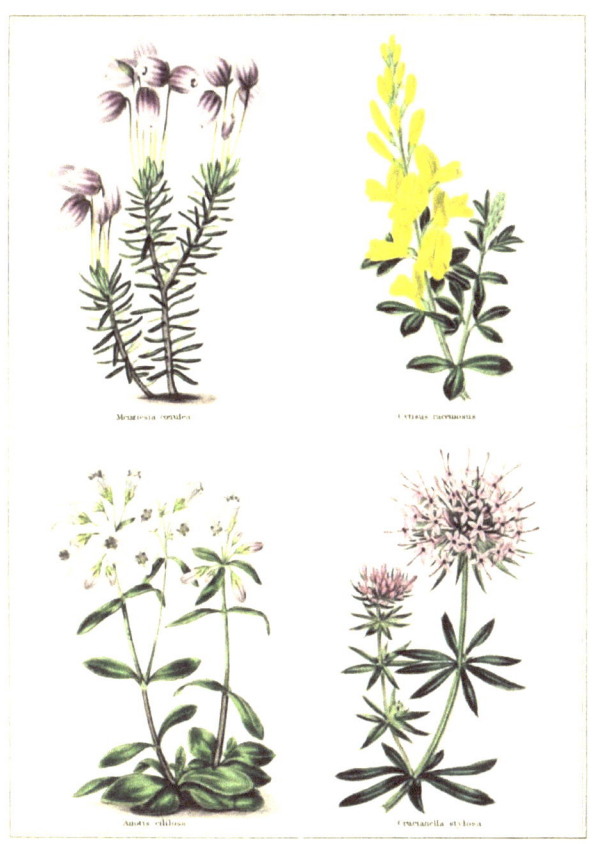

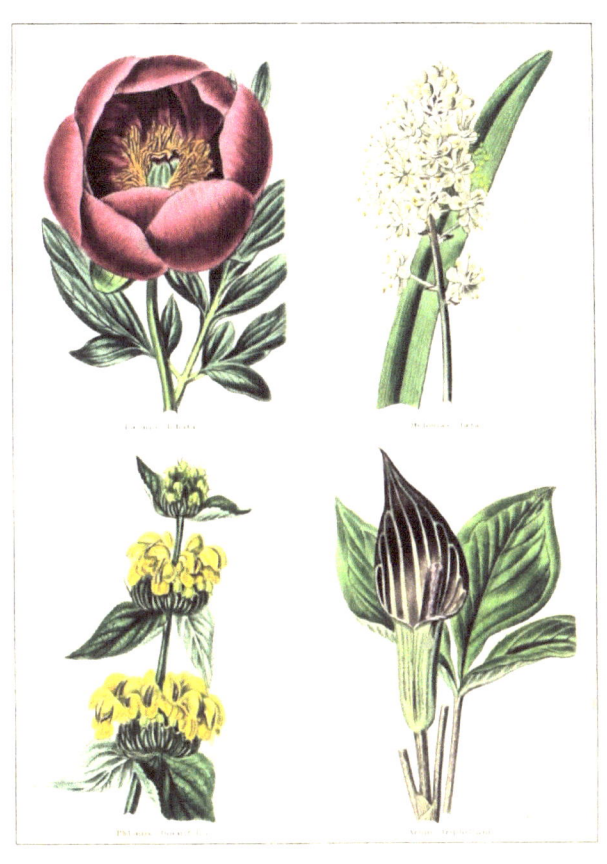

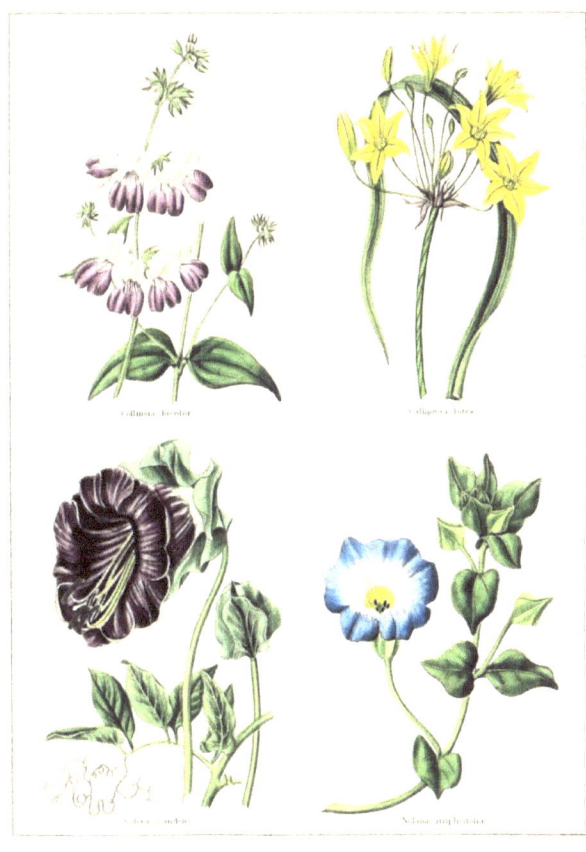

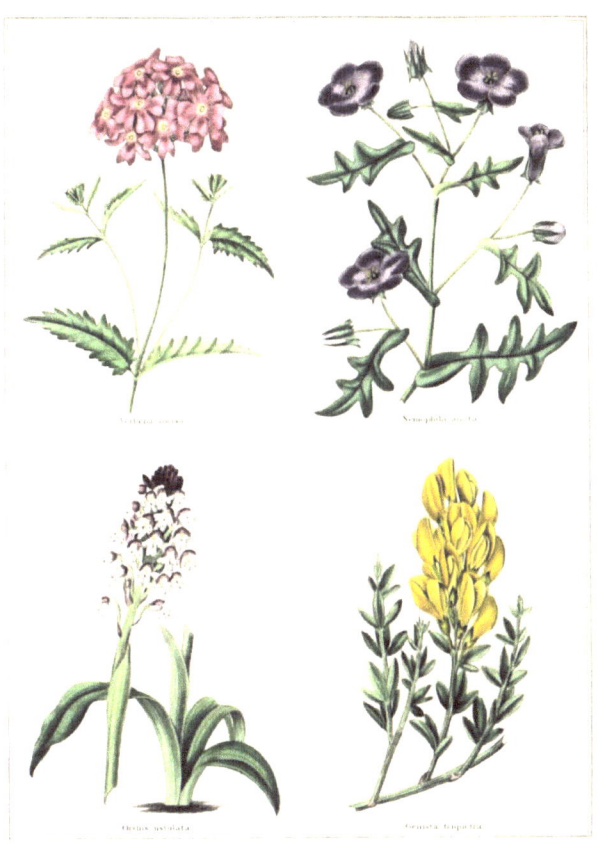

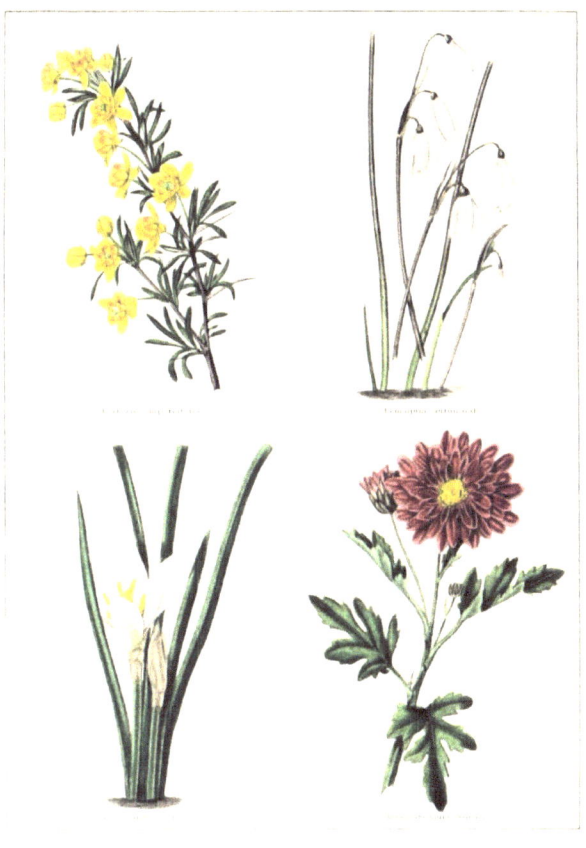